T0194998

Coffee & the Word

Geraldine Turner

WESTBOW
PRESS®
A DIVISION OF THOMAS NELSON
& ZONDERVAN

WestBow Press books may be ordered through booksellers or by contacting:

WestBow Press
A Division of Thomas Nelson & Zondervan
1663 Liberty Drive
Bloomington, IN 47403
www.westbowpress.com
844-714-3454

Because of the dynamic nature of the Internet, any web addresses or links contained in this book may have changed since publication and may no longer be valid. The views expressed in this work are solely those of the author and do not necessarily reflect the views of the publisher, and the publisher hereby disclaims any responsibility for them.

Any people depicted in stock imagery provided by Getty Images are models, and such images are being used for illustrative purposes only. Certain stock imagery © Getty Images.

Scripture marked (KJV) taken from the King James Version of the Bible.

Scripture quotations marked (NIV) are taken from the Holy Bible, New International Version®, NIV®. Copyright © 1973, 1978, 1984, 2011 by Biblica, Inc.® Used by permission of Zondervan. All rights reserved worldwide. www. zondervan.com The "NIV" and "New International Version" are trademarks registered in the United States Patent and Trademark Office by Biblica, Inc.®

ISBN: 978-1-6642-8733-4 (sc)
ISBN: 978-1-6642-8734-1 (hc)
ISBN: 978-1-6642-8735-8 (e)

Library of Congress Control Number: 2022923629

Print information available on the last page.

WestBow Press rev. date: 02/21/2023

I had thoughts of compiling a book of devotionals called *Coffee and the Word*, a very different devotional book. This book could be used for devotionals or sermons could result from it.

Study one devotion each day for a week. There are fifty-two devotions in the book. The reason is to get a person in the Word and the Word in the person. Do research, and entertain quiet thoughts from God, prayerfully, with inspiration. Get the Word on the particular devotion embedded in your mind and "think on these things" (Philippians 4:8 KJV). I recommend selecting a verse in the devotional to memorize each week.

Included are some helpful hints.

In these devotions, some of the scriptures are spaced throughout the devotion. Read them in their proper places since they go along with the comments. Certain words will be *italicized* for emphasis.

I dedicate this book to my husband, Reverend Harold Turner, who has been my supporter and encourager, with a listening ear.

~~~~~~

Thanks to Mrs. Cindy Pajak for her time and expertise in getting this book to the publisher.

TABLE OF CONTENTS

I WAS/AM BOUGHT

*R*EAD 1 Corinthians 6:19–20.

I am not my own—I am bought with a price, the supreme sacrifice of the life of Jesus; therefore, I must pay it forward, but how will I do that (Matthew 22:37 KJV)? Serve the Lord with my soul, mind, and strength. He will direct my path (Psalm 37:23 KJV). He will order my steps. It is up to me to follow the ordering. I do not know how to plan for myself (Proverbs 3:5–6; Romans 6:16). Because I was paid for by Jesus dying so I can live, the Word says I am to glorify (praise and worship) God in my body and in my spirit. There are several ways to glorify God: obey His Word and represent Him honorably to others, to name a few. How can I glorify God in my body (Romans 12:1 KJV)?

We should treat our bodies well since we are issued only one. Exercise, eat the right foods, get proper rest, and remain sexually pure. Remember, we are His hands and feet. Our bodies and minds are made to do good deeds.

Christ is living in me. Do I carry Him around dangerously or with love? He bought me; I owe Him.

PRAYER

God, I thank You for giving Jesus in my place. I ask You to help me to glorify You in my body and in my spirit. Jesus, I thank You for being the sacrifice for me. May I represent You respectfully since I carry Your name. I love You, and I thank You for loving me in such a demonstrative way.

A REFLECTION

*I*f I say I am a Christian, but my nature is not kind, loving, and caring, who am I reflecting? Surely not Christ. When I become a Christian and ask Jesus to live in my heart, I must take on His nature. If not, I could be misleading to others. Am I an embarrassment to the Christian name? Some people say, "If that is a Christian, I want no part of that."

Read 1 John 3:24 and Matthew 5:5–14, 48.

We should strive for perfection. We should be in complete conformity to God's laws, be broken in spirit, have a burden for others, and be meek and humble.

If I name the name of Christ, I must take on His attributes. I should not put on a show but exude His nature, be an extension of His love, and bring others to know Him. Are others interested in knowing Him because of my reflection?

Read 1 Corinthians 6:19–20 (this scripture is used in another devotion, and some of the same scriptures may be repeated throughout the book).

I must have a loving relationship with God; therefore, I will reflect Him in my actions because of my godly nature.

Read and study Luke 6:36, John 14:23, Ephesians 5:1, James 1:4, and 1 John 4:8, 16.

PRAYER

> Father, I thank You that I am in You and You are in me because of Jesus' sacrifice. Please teach me and caution me so that I can be a reflection You will be pleased with and so that people will want to know You for themselves.

KNOWING

A MADE-UP MIND WITH A GOAL is very important in the spiritual and secular worlds. I know who I am and whose I am. That gives me confidence. According to 2 Timothy 1:12, I have made the necessary arrangements to be in Christ. I know in whom I have believed and am persuaded.

With confidence I can model Him, but not with a "holier than thou" attitude. Everything I do should be with love. Am I perfect? No! Am I trying? Yes!

A model shows poise and walks with confidence. So should a model of Christ. I must walk with that confidence and talk with that confidence, but with meekness and not in a boastful way (Jude 1: 24–25). I must carry myself well and stand with confidence because I am modeling Him.

Study these scriptures: Galatians 5:1, 1 Corinthians 3:11, 1 Corinthians 16:13, 2 Timothy 2:19, and Isaiah 28:16.

A sure foundation promotes confidence in knowing.

Study these scriptures: Psalm 121:1–8, Matthew 7:7–11, and Philippians 4:19.

It is okay to talk with God verbally; then stop and read His Word, allowing it to fill in your spirit; and then talk to Him more. Read, meditate, listen, and pray.

PRAYER

God, I thank You that I can know You personally, and can trust in what You say. I am confident that You live in me and through me. You are my Father, and You want to provide the best for me.

CONDEMNATION

*D*o I CONDEMN MYSELF IN my judgment of others?

> "You, therefore, have no excuse, you who pass judgment on someone else, for at whatever point you judge the other, you are condemning yourself, because you who pass judgment do the same things. Now we know that God's judgment against those who do such things is based on truth. So, when you, a mere man, pass judgment on them and yet do the same things, do you think you will escape God's judgment?" (Romans 2:1–3 NIV)

Am I so blind to my faults and so ready to point out the faults of others that I cannot see myself clearly? According to verse 1, I am guilty of the same thing that I am judging someone else for. How easy is it to find fault with another?

People are different and come from different backgrounds.

Check the following scriptures: 2 Samuel 12:1–12, Matthew 7:1–5, Luke 6:37, and Romans 2:21–23.

PRAYER

> God, help me to stay focused on You and not on human frailties. I must remember we are all human beings subject to sins and faults. Help me to keep my goal in view and my focus on You. After all, I am not appointed to condemn and judge. I am called to serve.

WHY WORRY WHEN YOU CAN PRAY?

*W*ORRYING MAY BE THOUGHT OF as a "fix-it" tool, but the tool does not work. It just adds anxiety and stress to the nerves. When you are a fix-it person, it is hard to release the situation to God. I want to help Him, but what can I do? It has been said that prayer moves mountains, that prayer changes people, and that people change things (Philippians 4:6–7 KJV).

This is one of my favorite scriptures in the Bible because it has been real for me. My husband had some physical issues that I recognized were out of my hands, so worrying would not fix them.

The Word tells me not to be anxious for anything but to pray, ask my petition, and give thanks. God's peace, which is not really understood, will keep my heart and mind in perspective.

Worrying will not fix the problem, but I know who can; therefore, I must use my energy to talk with Him about it and express my faith.

Study the following scriptures: 1 Peter 5:6–7, Matthew 6:24–34, John 14:27, Isaiah 26:3, and Hebrews 12:2.[1]

So all of this comes down to trusting God.

PRAYER

> God, I love You and I thank You for Your love for me. You love me so much that You gave Your only begotten Son, Jesus, for me. I ask for forgiveness of my sins and shortcomings and for not trusting You as I should. I ask You to help me believe and trust You to the fullest extent (Psalm 68:19).

---

[1] Hebrews 12:2 gives us the antidote for worrying: loving and serving Jesus with thanks, putting faith and trust into practice, and remembering Romans 8:28.

TITHE

$\mathcal{R}$EAD MALACHI 3:6–12.

Am I known by God as a robber? If I do not pay tithes (God's money), that is exactly what I am, according to the scripture. These are sharp words (Proverbs 3:9–10 KJV).

Bring all the tithes. How much is all? Ten percent. I must honor God and return what is His to His storehouse. Some have asked, "What is the storehouse?" It is the church, or the house of God, where one is fed.

It is admirable to give to other ministries and missions beyond tithes, but I must remember if I have a need, most likely my church will address the need, not a ministry on television.

God says in His Word to prove or test Him to see if He will give me an abundant blessing. The results: God will rebuke or prevent the pests from destroying my crops, and He will bless me in my obedience to Him for blessing His house. On the other hand, if I do not give the tithe, I am under a curse. It has been said that God will get what is His. I choose to obey and be blessed.

If I use God's money, I am to repay it with an additional 20 percent. I do not want to owe God (Leviticus 27:31 KJV).

PRAYER

God, thank You for so many blessings—physical, spiritual, emotional, and financial. I do not want to withhold what I should give to You in any way. May I be obedient to Your Word in all things. Please bless me to be that cheerful giver.

A ROLLER COASTER RIDE

*R*EAD THE FOLLOWING SCRIPTURES: 1 Thessalonians 5:18, Philippians 4:11, 1 Corinthians 10:13, Psalm 34:19, and Luke 21:19.

In life, there are happy times, sad times, glad times, and bad times. Life is like a roller coaster ride with ups and downs, ins and outs, unpredictable turns, sudden stops, sharp curves, and sudden changes in speed and direction. There are times of thrills, suspense, exhilaration, and excitement. All these things cause fear, anxiety, faster breathing, a pounding heart, and an energy boost.

In life, we can go high, but we can also sink low. We are affected emotionally and physically. Life is like a roller coaster ride. You have probably been on this kind of ride at the fair. You knew there was a person operating the ride; the controls were in his hands. You, as a Christian, can recognize and compare your life to a roller coaster ride. There will be some high highs and some low lows, but you know who has the controls in His hands. This is when we keep our eyes on our destination, trusting the one in control.

Read Romans 8:28 and Hebrews 12:1–2.

PRAYER

God, I know life is not always a bed of roses. I want to praise You in the low times as well as the high times. You do not change, but You are the same. Help me to pattern my responses after You with sincere love and trust.

ADDICTED

*O*H NO, NOT I. AM I?

During the course of a lifetime, we can be addicted to many things. The mindset would imply drugs or alcohol. Addictions can cover so many things and these things can govern our lives. They may not be sinful things but can become as such if we let them separate us from God or rob us of time with Him (Isaiah 59:1–2 KJV).

Many things can be recognized as addictions if they become overpowering. A few are TV, computers, and cell phones. They can actually become thieves, to captivate our time, and to separate us from God, family, and friends.

Research these scriptures: Matthew 26:40 and Mark 14:37.

Today we could say, "Could I please enjoy your company, without a cell phone while we eat?" If not, you are saying to me, "I like being with you, but I favor my addiction over you." How rude is that?

There is a gospel song that says, "Love the people that God gives you, 'cause one day He'll want'em back." When time is lost, it cannot be found. Recognize true treasures and value them (Ephesians 5:15–16; Colossians 4:5).

Not all addictions are bad. It has been said if you practice something several days consecutively, it will become a habit. A habit can become an addiction. Reading the Bible and praying daily are great addictions. As stated earlier, a cell phone, a computer, and other activities can become addictions, but used wisely, can be helpful.

PRAYER

God, help me to keep all priorities in proper perspective so that when I call on You, I can have the confidence that You will hear me.

I WILL NOT FALL IF...

*H*AVE YOU EVER HAD THE dream of falling and you were glad to realize it was only a dream? Falling has never been fun, and as I get older, falling is not the thing to do. You may have watched a marathon when someone fell. Not only did it injure the person, the fall put the person behind (1 Corinthians 9:24 KJV). I do not want any injuries that can come with this mishap.

A few years ago, some of my friends and I went out of town to go shopping. That day, I took the worst fall I have ever had, and still have a knot to show for it. Falling is not the way to go.

Falling can happen physically, but a person can also fall spiritually, and that is definitely not wise or safe.

Read: 2 Thessalonians 2:1-3 1 Timothy 4:1–3 and Romans 12:3.

* *Faith*: Everyone should have a measure of faith, so we must add the following: 2 Peter 1:5–11.
* *Virtue:* Behavior showing high moral standards.
* *Knowledge:* Facts, information, and skills acquired by a person through experience or education.
* *Temperance:* Self-control.
* *Patience:* The ability to accept or tolerate delay, trouble, or suffering without getting upset.
* *Godliness:* Conforming to the laws and wishes of God.
* *Brotherly/Sisterly Kindness*: Extension of natural affection.
* *Charity:* The giving of love.

Study these eight attributes. According to the scripture, if a person possesses these, he or she will be rooted and grounded without falling.

PRAYER

God, I ask You to help me keep my eye on the prize
of Heaven and not be sidetracked by detours or any
attention-getters. I must persevere in this marathon,
remembering I am determined with a made-up mind.

Geraldine Turner

AN UNDERCOVER JOB

*R*EAD PSALM 121:1–8, PROVERBS 15:3, 1 Peter 5:6–7, John 14:21, Psalm 111:2, 2 Corinthians 4:17, Jeremiah 29:11, Isaiah 43:13, Nehemiah 13:2, and Psalm 46:10.

In the natural and spiritual worlds, we often experience uncomfortable situations. If we are serving God, we chose the right path. Our God does not sleep and is aware of everything that concerns us. He has His personal plan for each of us. Keep in mind Romans 8:28 (KJV). Even times that people have done things to harm us, He can turn them around for our good. I say that God works undercover.

A popular Christian contemporary song is so good at expressing some things we need to think on. The writer calls God a miracle worker, promise keeper, and light in the darkness, and He never stops working. How awesome is that for us? Listen to the song "Way Maker" by Sinach.

PRAYER

God, I thank You for daily blessings and Your provisions. I want to trust You completely since You know what is best for me. Your Word says that You order my steps, that You have plans for me, and that You will work for my good.

WHAT DOES GOD HATE?

IT HAS BEEN SAID SO many times that "God is love," and He is (John 3:16 KJV). God loved and does love in a great way, and He is so merciful. Could there be any hate found in God? Yes!

God hates six things and seven are abominations to Him (Proverbs 6:16–19 KJV).

1. A proud look (Psalm 101:5 KJV)
2. A lying tongue (Psalm 120:2 KJV)
3. Hands that shed innocent blood (Isaiah 1:15 KJV)
4. A heart that deviseth wicked imaginations (Genesis 6:5 KJV)
5. Feet that be swift in running to mischief (Isaiah 59:7) (Romans 3:15 KJV)
6. A false witness that speaketh lies (Psalm 27:12 KJV)
7. He that soweth discord among the brethren (Proverbs 6:14 KJV)

PRAYER

God, help me as I search my heart and mind on *all* these things. May I be more like You and less like the world. I want to align my life by Your Word.

I SHALL NOT BE MOVED

MOVED FROM WHAT? FROM SERVING God, from aiming for Heaven, and from living in God's tabernacle with Him. How can I avoid being moved?

Read Psalm 15:1–5 and Psalm 16:8.

* Walk and work righteousness.
* Speak truth.
* Do not talk about someone behind his or her back.
* Treat my neighbor kindly.
* Do not inflict harm or evil against my neighbor.
* Fear the Lord.
* Keep my oath.
* Do not illegally lend money at a very high rate of interest.
* Do not accept a bribe against the innocent.

"He that doeth these things shall never be moved" (Psalm 15:5b KJV).

An old song published in 1927 by Edward Boatner says, "I shall not be, I shall not be moved. I shall not be, I shall not be moved, just like a tree planted by the waters, I shall not be moved."

Another song that comes to mind about not being moved is "Keep on the Firing Line" by Bessie F. Hatcher, which says, "You must fight, be brave against all evil. Never run nor even lag behind. If you would win for God and the right, just keep on the firing line."

Read Galatians 6:9 and other scriptures on perseverance.

PRAYER

God, as I pray over each of the things listed in Psalm 15:1–5, help me to obey and conform to Your Word so I can live with You forever.

PRONOUNCE BLESSINGS

$\mathcal{R}$EAD GENESIS 48:1–22 (KJV). NOTICE verse 9, which reads, "Bring them, I pray thee, unto me, and I will bless them."

Read Genesis 27:1–4, 19, 25, and 31, Genesis 49:28, Deuteronomy 33:1, Hebrews 11:20 ("By faith Isaac blessed Jacob and Esau concerning things to come"), Proverbs 18:21, Matthew 12:36–37, Numbers 6:22–27, Psalm 19:14, Genesis 12:1–3, Proverbs 15:23, and Isaiah 50:4.

In biblical times, men pronounced blessings on their children, and it was like the blessings were set in stone. Pronouncing blessings on someone by faith can be powerful. Pronouncing cursings on someone can be detrimental. There is *power* in words. Speak words wisely and not in a careless way. We *must* pray and be more aware of how we speak to a person and what we speak over a person.

In biblical times and even today, mantles[2] are passed on to others. This reminds me of pronounced blessings. They both carry callings, anointings, and directions.

Read the following scriptures: 1 Kings 19:19–21, 2 Kings 2:8, 13, and 14, 1 Peter 4:10–11, and 1 Samuel 15:27.

PRAYER

> God, I ask for Your anointing and direction to speak uplifting and encouraging words to people. May I pronounce blessings upon them under Your authority and the anointing of the Holy Spirit.

---

[2] Mantles are symbols of sacrifice and commitment.

WHAT IS YOUR SIGN?

*T*HIS SOUNDS LIKE THE QUESTION is referring to a horoscope. No! No! Please do not go that way (Exodus 40:34–38).

The true story in the Bible of God's glory filling the temple and men not being able to stand is intriguing. I would like to bask in that (Leviticus 9:6, 23, and 24).

We know from the scriptures that the Israelites had clear directions or signs as to when to travel farther or stay. If the cloud was above them by day, they were to stay. When it lifted, they were to travel. At night, they could easily see where they should be since they had the pillar of fire (Exodus 13:21–22 KJV).

What is your sign to go forward? It may not be as distinct as the cloud and fire. It may be a slight nudge, a still small voice, or a leaning in a direction, but always in harmony with God's Word. Pray and follow (Isaiah 7:11 KJV, Psalm 37:23 KJV).

Clouds can be fascinating. Have you ever looked at clouds and named them by their shapes? Some might think they see Jesus or an angel in a cloud. Clouds are important. They announce coming rain and weather changes. Jesus will return with clouds (Revelation 1:7 KJV).

When my children were much younger, we were outside one day, and I called their attention to a particular cloud. I said, "That might be the cloud He's coming back on." Very quickly, my daughter apologized to her brother, saying, "I'm sorry, brother." Watch for the signs and go with the feelings as they agree with the Word.

PRAYER

God, I want to be close to You so I can feel Your direction for me. Help me to be very attentive.

ENCOURAGE YOURSELF

$\mathscr{R}$EAD 1 SAMUEL 30:1–6, 1 Samuel 23:16, Isaiah 25:1, Isaiah 26:3–4, and Psalm 56:1–13.

- I may be worried because of the way someone treats me.
- I may be brokenhearted because of the loss of a loved one.
- I may be depressed because I lost my job.
- I may be upset because of a physical diagnosis for me or someone I love.
- I may feel sadness that I cannot explain.

Whatever the case may be, I would say, "But there is God." I remember times He showed up for me in the past. You probably recall those times in your life. That is encouraging.

Read Psalm 62:7–8, Psalm 145:18, 2 Timothy 1:12, and 1 Peter 5:7.

This is the time I must rely on what I know from past experiences and draw on them with confidence. What He has done for others He will do for me.

A popular gospel song from years ago says "He'll Do It Again." (Dawn Thomas, writer) I am reminded of Hebrews 13:8 (KJV): "Jesus Christ the same yesterday, today, and forever."

PRAYER

God, when I think back over the past, I am reminded of times You came through for me. Psalm 46:1 (KJV) says, "God is our refuge and strength, a very *present help* in trouble." I trust You to work on my behalf.

DID I PROMISE?

I AM ONLY AS GOOD AS my word. When I make a promise to a person, usually he or she counts on my fulfilling that promise unless I let that person down in the past. I have heard people say that in the "olden days," a person was as good as his or her word. What has happened? Have people become too busy that they forget their promises?

What if we could not hold on to God's promises? Where would that put us? We are told in the Word that it is better not to make a vow than to make one and break it.

Read Numbers 23:19, Judges 11:29–40, James 4:13–17, James 5:12, Matthew 5:33–37, Colossians 3:9, and Colossians 4:6.

PRAYER

> God, I ask You to help me to fill my responsibilities—
> those things that are expected of me. Help me to hold
> true to my word and fill any promises that I have
> made in a satisfactory manner. I desire to keep my
> word as You keep Yours.

TRAIN UP A CHILD

*R*EAD GENESIS 18:19, DEUTERONOMY 6:1–9, Deuteronomy 11:19, Psalm 78:4, Ephesians 6:4, Colossians 3:21, 2 Timothy 3:14–15, and especially Proverbs 22:6.

The scripture does not say let a child find his or her way or make his or her own decisions. Sure, there are times they can make a decision on the kind of ice cream or candy he or she wants, but not life-changing decisions. That is why a child lives with his or her parents to receive training. The Word says to *train* the child. That is the awesome responsibility of the parents. It is actually a *command*. The Word does not say to train an adult. It says to *train a child*.

Development in a child happens in the first few years of his or her life. Different stages occur at different ages. It has been said that children develop habits by age nine. It seems that some do so even earlier.

Read Proverbs 20:7 and Proverbs 23:24.

Parents who train their children in the nurture and admonition of the Lord reap benefits. There is no guarantee that their children will never go astray. If we have trained them, then we refer again to the promise in Proverbs 22:6 and hold on to it. God's promises never fail.

PRAYER

> God, I thank You that I was brought up in a Christian home and taught Your Word. Thank You for my children and grandchildren, and I ask for Your blessings, direction, protection, and anointing be upon them.

LAY IT OUT BEFORE THE LORD

*R*EAD ISAIAH 37:1–38. NOTICE VERSE 14.

We have various needs: spiritual, physical, mental, emotional, social, and financial. Hezekiah literally spread the problem before the Lord that concerned him.

Read 1 Peter 5:6–7, Psalm 55:22, and Luke 12:22–32.

Just as Hezekiah took the step to get God's attention on a worrisome matter, we should do the same. We can literally lay it out before the Lord and tell Him our concern. It may be pictures of loved ones, letters, or other things. Take that step as a "faith-builder" to get in touch with God.

"And all things, whatsoever ye shall ask in prayer, believing, ye shall receive" (Matthew 21:22 KJV).

Read Psalm 138:8.

We should bring our needs before the Lord. It is good to follow the acronym ACTS.

A	Adoration (Praise)
C	Confession (Repentance)
T	Thanks (Thanksgiving)
S	Supplication (Requests)

PRAYER

God, help me to realize You love me so much that You care about what concerns me. Hebrews 4:16 (KJV) says, "Let us therefore come boldly unto the throne of grace, that we may obtain mercy and find grace to help in time of need."

RULED OUT OF HEAVEN (1)

*T*HE FOLLOWING ARE CLASSIFIED AS wicked people who will not inherit Heaven. Do you know of any people who might be in these categories?

> Sexually immoral people
> Idolaters
> Adulterers
> Male prostitutes
> Homosexual offenders
> Thieves
> Greedy people
> Drunkards
> Slanderers
> Swindlers

Check these out with the following scriptures: Galatians 5:19–21, 1 Corinthians 6:9–10, Ephesians 5:5, 1 Timothy 1:9–10, and Psalm 101:3–8.

We might have a tendency to think that some on this list are not as bad as others.

In a devotional, we like to feel lifted up and encouraged. There are times the truth needs to be revealed for our own good. After all, who wants to be deceived? Who wants to go into life or death blindly?

There is no way to get around the elimination of those who will not make Heaven. God knows who He wants in His Kingdom. Make the right choice for yourself.

PRAYER

God, my ultimate goal is Heaven. I want others to go also. Please help me to not condemn others for their lifestyles, but to love them and show them You. I want to help them through Your Word. My word will not make the difference.

Geraldine Turner

RULED OUT OF HEAVEN (2)

*L*ISTED ARE SCRIPTURES REPEATING SOME of the sins that were mentioned in the previous devotion.

> Genesis 1:27–28 (male and female)
> Leviticus 18:1–30
> Leviticus 20:13
> Matthew 19:9
> Mark 10:11–12
> James 1:13–15

The above scriptures list/deal with those who will not make Heaven, unless there is repentance. Furthermore, a person can be a good moral person, not committing any horrible sin, and be ruled out of Heaven. It takes repenting and accepting Jesus as Lord and Savior to not miss Heaven. That was His purpose for dying (Romans 5:12).

As I make my choices, I must be sure they are scripturally sound. I will be justified or condemned by God's Word.

PRAYER

> God, help me to be free from these sins, and strive to be more like You. I love You and I appreciate Your Word, which is a guide for me. I realize I should live according to Your Word, because I will be judged by it.

AM I A HYPOCRITE?

$\mathscr{R}$EAD MARK 7:6–7, ISAIAH 29:13, Ezekiel 33:31, and Matthew 15:8–9.

Because of my daily pattern of praying, I have found that I need to be careful to pay attention to what I am praying and mean it from the heart. After so many times of going through a ritual or habit, a person can proceed in it without giving it the heartfelt emotion.

Have you ever prayed for someone in his or her presence because it was expected of you but the feeling did not come from the heart? Maybe you were just filling a duty.

Read James 5:16.

There are different ways a person can be a hypocrite. Could insecurity be one of those? We should do everything with love and sincerity, as the Word says, in order to get results.

Read 1 Corinthians 16:14.

PRAYER

God, I want to pray from the heart in order to touch You with my concerns that are _____.

THE GLORY OF THE LORD

*R*EAD EZEKIEL 43:1–5. NOTICE THESE words in this passage.

"the way of the east"
"glory of the Lord"
"through the gate"
"inner court"
Ezekiel 44:4 North Gate
Ezekiel 10:19 East Gate
Ezekiel 11:23 Glory on the East Side
1 Kings 8:10–11 Holy Place, glory
2 Chronicles 5:13–14 In one accord, glory
2 Chronicles 7:1–2 Glory

I read in these and other scriptures about the glory of the Lord filling the house, and I am in awe. The people *could not stand* in God's presence. He *is* omnipotent (all powerful), omniscient (all knowing), and omnipresent (present everywhere).

God's Spirit entered from specific directions. In the above scriptures, it was the East Gate and North Gate. Notice He entered through the gate and did not just appear. His presence was in the Inner Court, the Holy Place.[3]

How can we experience this? Worship Him in one mind, in one accord, and with one purpose. Can I experience this if I am alone in worship? Yes, by focusing on Him, loving Him, and listening. There is song that says, "Let us come into His presence with thanksgiving in our hearts and give Him praise, and give Him praise." (Don Moen, writer) Sometimes it can be energizing to have quiet worship music on when I pray.

---

[3] God can appear wherever He chooses.

PRAYER

God, Your Word says, "In Thy presence is fullness of joy." I would like to bask in Your presence. Help me to worship You for Who You are and not for what You can do for me. *I want to experience Your glory.*

Geraldine Turner

PSALM 23

ONE OF THE MOST POPULAR scriptures is the twenty-third Psalm. The "attention-getters" in this passage are the adjectives. For example, in verse 2, He makes me to lie down, not just in pastures, but in *green* pastures. He leads me beside the *still* (calm) waters. Verse 3 says, He leads me not in any path, but in *righteous* paths for His name's sake. Take notice of verse 4: "Yea though I walk through the valley of the shadow of death, I will fear no evil: for Thou art with me; Thy rod and Thy staff they comfort me." There are valleys I have to walk through, but not alone. I do not have to camp out in the valley but walk through it, knowing God is with me. A natural valley is described as an elongated low area, often running between hills or mountains and that may contain a river or stream. These can be compared to the Christian walk: valley, hill, mountain, and river.

God will be with me as I walk. After all, He wants the best for me. He gives me green pastures, still waters, and righteous paths, to name a few.

As one continues to travel, he or she will not stay in the valley (Psalm 30:5). Remember, *the stream in the valley can be refreshing.*

PRAYER

God, I thank You for being my Shepherd, and for watching over me. This gives me peace of mind and contentment. Your Word tells me that You walk with me. I do have valleys to go through and You are right beside me in the valleys. I realize the "valley experiences" can help me climb higher. You know what is best for me. I want to trust You.

FAITH WITHOUT WORKS IS DEAD

*R*EAD JAMES 2:14–26. NOTICE VERSES 21 and 22.

Faith and works go hand-in-hand. Abraham was told to offer Isaac. Abraham was obedient, and followed through with God's command, with faith.

Read Genesis 22:1–14. In verses 5 and 8, Abraham showed his faith and trust, along with his works.

Read Joshua 2:1–24 and Joshua 6:25.

I have had people say to me they are praying about some issues. I said, "There are some prayers you need to put legs under." Prayers can be looked on as faith, sometimes, but actions are works. James 1:22 (KJV) says, "But be ye doers of the Word, and not hearers only, deceiving your own selves."

There are some things you can pray about until you are blue in the face, but some of these things may take action or work on our parts.

God gave to each one a measure of faith. Faith is comparable to muscles: the more they are exercised, the stronger they become.

Personal testimonies of prayers answered are "faith builders." True life experiences are proven facts (Romans 10:17).

PRAYER

> God, I thank You for the measure of faith that You gave me. I am sorry for any unbelief. Since faith comes by hearing Your Word, I must dedicate myself to Your Word to increase my faith.

DID I COMMIT MURDER?

*R*EAD MATTHEW 5:21–22, 1 JOHN 3:15, and 1 John 4:20.

Two of the Ten Commandments are "Thou shalt not kill" and "Thou shalt not bear false witness against thy neighbor" (Exodus 20:13 and 16 KJV) If I have hatred or bad feelings toward someone, I could talk to someone else about that person. In doing so, I can hurt that person's influence, so where does that raise me to? It does not! Digging dirt puts me lower in the dirt.

Study and *meditate* on these scriptures: Provers 26:27, Psalm 140:1–3, Psalm 141:3, Proverbs 13:3, and Proverbs 21:23.

Where do murderers fit in with God's plan? Not in Heaven!

The tongue is an unruly member.

Read James 3:8, Proverbs 18:21, Matthew 5:11, and Mark 12:31.

PRAYER

> God, help me to guard what I say, bless people, and not curse them in my actions. I know You love others as much as You love me. May I love them and pray for them in their faults.

HOW TO PROSPER

"This is what Hezekiah did throughout Judah, doing what was good and right and faithful before the Lord his God. In everything that he undertook in the service of God's temple and in obedience to the law and the commands, he sought his God and worked whole heartedly. And so, he *prospered*." (2 Chronicles 31:20–21 NIV)

*R*EAD 2 KINGS 20:3, 2 Kings 22:2, 2 Chronicles 26:5, 2 Chronicles 32:30, Psalm 1:3, Psalm 41:1–3, Matthew 6:33, and Ecclesiastes 9:10. The above Scriptures give us examples of ways to *prosper*.

Seek God with the whole heart.
Walk in truth with a perfect heart.
Stay on course.
Delight in God's law.
Consider the poor.
Do everything with love.
Whatever I find to do, do it with all my might.

This is God's plan for you and me (John 3:2).

An entrepreneur does not want to pay a worker for doing a job halfway. We would not think of stealing from the company. Would we think of being lazy on the job and not giving it our best? What is the difference? We must do things well, right, and truthfully, with all our might, heart, and dedication. That is the way to earn payment and benefits.

PRAYER

God, I want to dedicate myself to You in love and trust, knowing You will work all things for my good. I understand that You want me to *prosper* in every way. Please guide and help me in this dedication.

WHY SUICIDE?

$\mathcal{I}$F WE GO AGAINST THE longing of the soul, which is made to inhabit God, then there is conflict. The soul is hungry and thirsty for God. Read the following scriptures: Psalm 42:2, Psalm 63:1, Psalm 84:2, Psalm 143:6, Isaiah 55:1, Matthew 5:6, John 6:35, John 4:14, and John 10:10.

Satan's purpose is to steal, kill, and destroy. He does it through afflicting the body and mind. When we listen to him, we become weak and fall into his trap. Many times, people lose their senses toward the Holy Spirit, and Satan takes control of the soulish nature. This does not mean he has control of our spirits. Satan uses every natural power to gain control of our minds, and the end is detrimental.

I do not know all the answers concerning the topic, but I know the answer for some people. There have been Christians who have committed suicide. The thought in the past was that if a person did this, he or she automatically went to hell. We cannot read the heart to know the actual condition of a person and what he or she deals with. Jesus is the judge; therefore, we leave it up to Him. He is just.

Some people are known to have chemical imbalances; some suffer from trauma and other conditions. To answer the topic for sinners: souls have longings that many do not know about. They are searching in so many places for things to satisfy that desire. Many people feel unfulfilled, experience a void, and have a lack of purpose. This is the time for the Christian to introduce a person to Jesus.

PRAYER

> God, help me to be the link that connects someone to You, to satisfy hunger and thirst. I realize many are searching and do not know for what. Help me to direct those people to you.

WITNESS TO THAT LOST ONE

*P*EOPLE RESPOND TO LIFE STORIES. That is why it is effective for a person to share his or her own story of meeting Jesus as the personal Savior. Remember, it is good to tell the person that each person has a soul and that soul desires God's residence.

Read Revelation 3:20.

Jesus will enter the heart/soul by invitation *only*. Explain to the one you witness to that Adam and Eve sinned, so we are born into sin.

Read Romans 3:23, Romans 6:23, and Hebrews 9:27.

Jesus died for us so that we can live with Him eternally (Romans 10:9–10).

Pray and ask for God's direction to witness and minister to each individual. Be sensitive to the Holy Spirit. People are different.

PRAYER

> Jesus, I ask You to forgive me of my sins and to come into my heart to live. I thank You for suffering and dying for me. I believe God raised You from the dead, and You are alive forevermore. *Hallelujah!*

SET FREE BY AN EARTHQUAKE

*R*EAD ACTS 16:14–40.

Many times, in our lives blessings seem to come in disguises, and sometimes tough disguises. God's ways are not our ways (Isaiah 55:8–9). Actually, if He had chosen, He could have prevented Paul and Silas from being put into prison. Sometimes our trials are not only for us; others can be affected, as well. God works "full circle" and not just for you and me.

Your trial might be an imprisonment, an earthquake, a dungeon, a misunderstanding, or a rebuke. However, the very thing that binds you may be the instrument used to set you free. That was the case with the earthquake in Acts 16:26. Doors were opened and chains were loosed. This freedom took place after Paul and Silas prayed and sang praises.

God is pleased with our praises. It has been said that He inhabits the praises of His people (Psalm 22:3 KJV). When we give Him real praises from the heart, God can move mountains for us. There is a gospel song by Teddy Huffam that says, "God will bankrupt heaven to meet my need."

PRAYER

God, I love You and praise You for Your love for me, so unconditional and so real. I thank You because You have my best interest at heart and want what is best for me. I believe if I love, serve, and follow You the best I can, You will open doors for me just as you did for Paul and Silas.

WHO OR WHAT IS YOUR ISAAC?

*R*EAD GENESIS 22:1–14. REMEMBER THE story in the Bible?

God told Abraham to take his son, Isaac to Moriah and offer him for a burnt offering. That would be quite a test, especially since Isaac was a promised child. Abraham obeyed. He saddled the donkey, and took Isaac, two young men, and the wood for a burnt offering with him. "Abraham staggered not at the promise of God" (Romans 4:17–21 KJV). His obedience overpowered any fear. His trust prevailed. He told the young men to stay with the donkey while he and Isaac went up the mountain to worship. What amazing faith and trust Abraham had in his God. God knew what Abraham would do, but Abraham proved to himself his reliance on God. What a testimony! God did provide a ram, just in time (Matthew 6:33).

Abraham's great love for his promised child was tried and he came through victorious. He had to obey to come to a greater blessing. Who or what is your Isaac, a dearly beloved being or thing? Is it between you and God or is it placed just under God? It could be so easy to hold on to a person, a habit, or ritual that puts God in second place.

Trust God and step out. After all, He wants the best for us.

Read 1 Samuel 15:22 and Matthew 6:33.

How willing are we to sacrifice for a greater blessing?

PRAYER

> God, help me to not have other gods before You. I know You are the one, true God who loves me and proves that love for me. Thank You for the sacrifice. May I have You in first place in my life and then other things will line up in order.

GOD'S ON-TIME PROVISION

*R*EMEMBER THE PREVIOUS DEVOTION "WHO or What Is Your Isaac?" God provided the ram, the sacrifice to be used in the place of Isaac (Genesis 22:14). Jehovah-Jireh means "our Provider."

There are times we pray for financial needs as well as physical, spiritual, and emotional needs. God does not always answer in our timing. His timing can be different.

I saw a card that got my attention. It had a picture of a cat hanging onto a knot in a rope. That is an expression of how people feel sometimes when it seems our answers are delayed.

If I love God above all else, and if I am called according to His purpose, then *I will trust Him* to work things out for my good; therefore, He knows when to come through for me in provision.

Read Romans 8:28, Matthew 6:33, Philippians 4:19, Psalm 23:1, 2 Corinthians 9:8, and Psalm 145:18–19.

PRAYER

> God, I thank You for provisions in the past. You have blessed me in so many ways, every day (Psalm 68:19 KJV). "Blessed be the Lord, Who *daily* loadeth us with benefits, even The God of our salvation." I bring to You my need (specify the need) and I ask for Your *provision* and answer to this need.

ALL CREATION SHOULD PRAISE THE LORD

*R*EAD PSALM 148:1–14. CHECK OUT a list of some who should praise the Lord.

Angels: "Let everything that hath breath praise the Lord.

Heavenly Hosts: "Praise ye the Lord" (Psalm 150:6 KJV).

Sun

Moon: How can we praise Him? Read Psalm 149:3–4 KJV for other ways.

Stars

Heavens: All people and things should praise the Lord. If not, "I tell you that, if these should hold their peace, the stones would immediately cry out" (Luke 19:40 KJV).

Waters

Sea Creatures

Fire

Hail

Snow

Vapor

Stormy wind

Mountains

Hills

Fruitful trees

Cedars

Beasts

Cattle

Creeping things

Flying fowl
Kings
People
Princes
Judges
Young men
Maidens
Old men
Children

Read Psalm 145:1.

PRAYER

God, I do thank and praise You for what You do.
You are worthy to be praised for Who You are. You
have the name above all names. You are the *one* true
God, Creator of Heaven and Earth, and God of the
universe. It is no wonder that your creation should
praise You.

AM I RESPONSIBLE FOR THE STORM?

*D*ID MY DISOBEDIENCE CAUSE DISCOMFORT for others? First Samuel 15:22–23 (KJV) says, "Obedience is better than sacrifice." Read Jonah chapters one through three.

Jonah disobeyed and tried to get away from God's presence, thus causing a dangerous storm. He could not get away from God's presence and neither can we. If Jonah had obeyed God's order for him to go to Ninevah, he would have prevented a storm. "The eyes of the Lord are in every place, beholding the evil and the good" (Proverbs 15:3 KJV).

"For the gifts and calling of God are without repentance" (Romans 11:29 KJV). Obedience is the best way to go to avoid some unnecessary storms. After all, God knows our end from the beginning. He knows the steps He will order for us. I must trust Him since he works all things for my good. I do not know my future; He does.

The men on the ship did not want to pay for Jonah's disobedience with their lives (Jonah 1:14).

Have I made decisions that greatly affected people's lives? Did I put them in unnecessary storms because I did not follow God's direction for me? Am I responsible for the storm?

PRAYER

> God, help me to follow You closely so I will make right decisions for me, and for those who will be affected by my decisions. I pray that I will not be spiritually deaf, but hear Your direction and follow through.

THE LORD'S SUPPER

*T*AKING PART IN COMMUNION, ALSO known as the Lord's Supper, is a very serious act (1 Corinthians 11:24–30). Jesus said to remember Him when we take part, because we show His death until He comes. We take part in this *only* if we have been forgiven of our sins and Jesus lives in our hearts. He enters by invitation *only* (2 Corinthians 13:5 and Revelation 3:20).

If we take part and have not met these requirements, we are guilty of crucifying Jesus (Hebrews 6:6). If so, we also drink damnation with judgment on ourselves. As a result, many people have been sick and even died. We *must* examine ourselves always before taking communion, to be sure our sins are under the blood. If we are not sure about things in our lives, *now* is the time to ask for forgiveness.

When some churches serve communion, they also wash each other's feet. Read about this in John 13:1–17.

Through Jesus' death, we can have life forever. "For the bread of God is He which cometh down from Heaven and giveth life unto the world" (John 6:33 KJV). We take the bread, which represents Jesus' body, and the grape juice, which represents His blood.

Jesus gave the *ultimate sacrifice* for us. He received agony, torture, rejection, ridicule, pain, and suffering for Himself, for His mom, and others who loved Him. What a sacrifice He made for me! I must thank Him personally.

PRAYER

God, I thank You for giving Your only Son for me, knowing how He would have to suffer. Jesus, I thank You for being my *sacrifice*, for my sins, for my healing, and for total deliverance. I love You (John 6:51).

A POINT OF CONTACT

$\mathcal{R}$EAD MARK 5:27–30, MATTHEW 9:20–22, and Matthew 14:34–36.

The woman with the issue of blood spent all she had and got worse. She had her eye on Jesus, who was her answer. She made her way through the crowd, keeping her eye on Jesus, her aim and goal. Her mindset was that she *must* touch Him who was her hope and her faith. Jesus felt virtue (power) leave His body when she touched Him (Acts 3:16). She felt healing in her body. *There was a transfer.* When Jesus questioned who touched Him, the woman was afraid because she had taken something from Jesus (Mark 5:33). She told Jesus all the truth. She touched only the hem of His garment. Touching Jesus is what it is about.

Years ago, evangelist Oral Roberts taught people to have a point of contact, which can serve as a spark of faith. Let your faith be there when you touch that object.

Equation: Point of Contact (touch) + Faith = the Answer

On a personal note, people in the community knew that my parents would pray for their needs when they went to them with the requests. I saw how this worked in telling the people of how God had answered prayers so many times. These were faith builders. So many times, Daddy would know someone needed prayer and he would say so. There were times that he would be sick and get relief after someone came for prayer. Even sometimes, he would pray for people, after which the fever from them would be in his hand. That was a prayer of contact along with faith.

Remember, faith and works go together.

PRAYER

God, thank You for the measure of faith that You gave me and I want it to grow. I desire to witness Your miracles. Help me so that when I reach out and touch, the *point of contact* will be made successfully.

THEY HATE ME

$\mathcal{R}$EAD LUKE 6:22–23.

Hate is a *strong* word. Why would anyone hate me? I try to live a godly life, identifying as a Christian.

I have known of people in the presence of Christians who feel condemnation. The Holy Spirit in a child of God can make the spirit in a sinner uncomfortable, and the Christian does not have to say anything in a condemning manner. Two different spirits can collide and react. Even if the blood of Jesus is mentioned around a person who is demon possessed, that person sometimes reacts.

If someone who is not serving God is in your presence, or maybe he or she lost that first love (Jesus), condemnation overrides (Revelation 2:4). That person wants to exclude you from his or her presence because he or she is uncomfortable. The person may even insult you or talk to other people about you, trying to use his or her influence. That is murder.

The Word says to *rejoice* (James 1:2 KJV). When you suffer wrongfully, just remember that you are not the only one (Matthew 5:11 and 1 Peter 2:19). Carry yourself, be faithful to God, and you will not be sorry. That person may come to you in the future and ask for forgiveness. Take confidence in knowing *who you are* and *whose you are. Stand firm*—it will pay off!

P R A Y E R

God, I want to serve You and conform to Your will and Your way. I do not ever want to deny You, but stand firm for You, no matter the persecution. You tell me in James 1:2 KJV to count it all joy when I have different trials. I know the best is yet to come (2 Timothy 2:12).

THERE WILL BE A RETURN (ON YOUR DEEDS)

*R*EAD ACTS 10:4, PROVERBS 19:17, 2 Corinthians 9:6–8, Luke 6:38, Matthew 7:12, and Galatians 6:7.

God takes notice and keeps record of one who helps the poor and obeys in giving blessings to others. It has been said that Christians can be conduits or channels. After all, we are God's hands and feet. It is exciting and does the heart good when reaching out to someone while not expecting anything. There are many ways to do this. For example:

* Paying for the food for the one behind you in line;
* Giving to someone you observe in the checkout line at the grocery store who moves to put items back;
* Babysitting for a mom who needs a break;
* Blessing a caregiver;
* Making a meal for a family;
* Taking someone to the doctor; or
* Many more charitable acts.

All of these are ways to bless others. Giving to the poor absolutely gets God's attention. The scripture tells us that giving to the poor is making a loan to God.

Acts 10:4 (KJV) says, "Thy prayers and thine alms are come up for a memorial before God." God knows the sincere prayers we pray for others and how we bless them. The bottom line is this: we will reap what we sow, according to the Word. *There will be a return.*

PRAYER

God, help me to be Your eyes, hands, and feet to minister to others. Please direct me to those in need, and bless me so I can bless others in Jesus' name.

CHARGE MY HEART—
THE PHONE CAN WAIT

$\mathcal{R}$EAD ABOUT SAMSON IN JUDGES 16:1–22. He knew where his strength was but let down his guard. He went to Gaza, met a prostitute, and spent the night with her. When the people of Gaza found out Samson was there, they surrounded the place and waited to kill him. They were not able to do so.

Later, Samson fell in love with Delilah. The rulers of the Philistines wanted her to find out the secret of his strength. They offered to give her money for the information. He fooled her with three stories. "If you love me, you will tell me." How familiar is this today? "If you love me, you will" do what is asked. Samson was a Nazarite and his hair had never been cut. On the fourth try, the secret was revealed. His hair was cut, and he lost his strength. He awoke and said, "I will go out as at other times before, and shake myself," but his strength was gone. The Philistines took him, put his eyes out, and put him to work.

What happened here? First of all, he was in places and with people he should not have been. This caused much suffering after losing his strength. He needed to keep his heart charged, daily, in the right place. So should we.

In 1 Corinthians, chapter 15, verse 31 (KJV), Paul said, "I die daily." He may have been referring to circumstances with animals, but I tend to think of this for ourselves as Christians. We should go to the cross daily, repent, be charged, renewed, and revived. Then, when evil comes our way, we will recognize the devil's tactics. We usually charge our phones daily so our contact will not be hindered. How much more important is it to charge our hearts daily, so our contact, Jesus, will not be hindered?

The *real* in us identifies the false that comes to us. Do not lose strength participating in vain things. We must *keep our hearts charged*.

PRAYER

God, I want to renew daily with You, to stay in line.
I need that freshness of the Spirit that comes just as
Your mercies are new every morning.

Geraldine Turner

TAKE A STAND

$\mathcal{R}$EAD 1 KINGS 19:1–18.

I attended a relatively small school, and in high school, I had the mindset that I was the only Christian there, but I probably was not. I did stand up for my convictions and my classmates knew that. I was not a loud, outspoken person, but my beliefs were important to me. Pleasing Jesus was first and foremost.

Read John 7:1-13 (take note of verse 13) and John 12:42–43.

The Pharisees did not want to confess Jesus openly. Is this a problem with some people today (Mark 8:38; Luke 9:26)? The reason could be that Jesus is not known to be the most popular subject today.

Dedication and proclamation comes in knowing who I am in Him and whose I am for Him. This was also stated in the devotion "Knowing."

Sometimes it may feel like you are the only one on God's side, but possibly not. This is a critical time. When have we ever known the world to be in such turmoil as it is today? We must *take a stand*. Our lives and deaths depend on it.

Read Ephesians 6:10–20, 1 Corinthians 15:58, 1 Corinthians 16:13, Philippians 1:27, Philippians 4:1, and 1 Peter 5:9.

PRAYER

God, my Father, I never want to deny You, no matter the opposition. Help me to stand firm, with my eye on the goal, and never waiver. I can be strong because You are with me.

DO ALL THINGS WITH LOVE

*R*EAD 1 CORINTHIANS 16:14 AND 1 Peter 4:8.

Do all things with love, whether handing something to someone, cleaning behind someone, taking up someone's slack, being a caretaker, or any number of things. I must remember I am God's hands and feet. I must represent God's grace and mercy.

Two great commandments are in Matthew 22:37–39.

According to Proverbs 17:17, a friend loves at all times, even when getting on the nerves.

According to Matthew 5:44, I must love my enemies.

According to John 15:13, I must love, even though I can be irritated and aggravated at the time.

What if God blessed us only when we are loving, kind, and nice? You have heard the saying, "Grin and bear it." Do not respond with retaliation, but with *love*. Jesus expressed the ultimate love when He lay down His life to take care of our sins. *That is love.*

PRAYER

Jesus, You and Your Father set the perfect example of love. Help me to see people through Your eyes, spiritually, and not through my natural eyes only. You displayed the ultimate love. May I strive to do the same. Thank You for Your love."

WORTHY OF THE VOCATION (CALLING)

$\mathcal{E}$ PHESIANS 4:1 (KJV) SAYS, "I therefore, the prisoner of the Lord, beseech you that ye walk worthy of the vocation wherewith ye are called."

First Thessalonians 2:1 (KJV) says, "That ye would walk worthy of God, Who hath called you unto His kingdom and glory."

Matthew 22:14 (KJV) says, "For many are called but few are chosen."

Do we ever feel worthy of the calling God has placed on us? We are not worthy within ourselves, but God knows how He can equip us, and how we can do this for Him. Read Romans 11:29. We should trust God's judgment and calling, since He knows what is best for us and what the final product will be.

Read Numbers 23:19. We should obey.

Read Romans 12:1.

How can I prepare myself to be worthy of my calling? With Jesus in my heart, I just dedicate and present myself to Him with no reservations, making His will my ultimate goal. Remember Romans 8:28 and Matthew 6:33. God has an order for us (Psalm 37:23).

You may feel God has been calling you to a specific work. You may be using talents that promote that work. Talk to God about this and listen to His directions.

It is an honor to be called to represent God, especially since Jesus represented us.

PRAYER

God, I want to obey the calling You have on my life.
While serving in this calling, I will be with people
who will make an impact on my life. Help me to hear
You clearly and follow You closely.

GOD'S GOT YOUR BACK

*S*ECOND THESSALONIANS 1:6 (KJV) SAYS to "recompense tribulation to them that trouble you." God is the Father. Sometimes parents punish a child for picking on a sibling.

Psalm 103:13 (KJV) says, "Like as a father pitieth his children, so the Lord pitieth them that fear Him." Is this not pretty much the same as with parents?

Read the following scriptures: Galatians 6:7, Proverbs 22:8, and Job 4:8–9.

It may be hard sometimes for us to keep accurate records, but God does that on us. He is very aware of our actions and our hearts. Being the Father, He knows when to chastise, and when to give a pat on the back.

Read the following scriptures: Jeremiah 17:10, Jeremiah 32:19, and Psalm 62:12.

Seek God, serve Him, keep Him the main one, and allow Him to deal with the tribulators. *God's got your back*; after all, He is the Father.

PRAYER

> God, I know You love all people, Your creations. Help me to see them, and even my enemies, through Your eyes. Your Word tells me to pray for those who despitefully use me. I ask for Your blessings on them in Jesus' name, knowing that You will bless me as well.

THE HEART REVEALS

$\mathcal{R}$EAD 1 SAMUEL 16:1–13. ESPECIALLY take note of verse 7.

Read Psalm 147:10–11 and Proverbs 9:10.

Humans see only the outside—the actions and reactions. God knows the heart and its actions and reactions.

Read the following scriptures: 1 Kings 8:38–40, 1 Chronicles 28:9, Jeremiah 17:10, Psalm 7:9, 1 Corinthians 14:25, Proverbs 17:3, and Romans 8:27.

We may think that we have things hidden, but whatever is in the heart can manifest at inopportune times.

Several of these scriptures tell that God searches the heart and knows what is there. It is up to me to search my heart daily and be sure it is in alignment with God. Life flows from the physical and spiritual heart. Without the heart, I am dead.

Let your prayer be these scriptures: Psalm 139:23–24 and Psalm 51:10.

FINISHED

$\mathcal{E}$XODUS 40:1–38 DEALS WITH SETTING up the Tabernacle, according to God's plan and design. Aaron, his sons, and items were to be washed, anointed, and sanctified. The men were to wear holy garments.

Things in the Tabernacle were set in order (Exodus 40:17–33). Notice verse 33. Moses *finished* the work. *Then* the *glory* of the Lord appeared (verses 34 through 38).

First Corinthians 14:40 (KJV) says, "Let all things be done decently and in order." We, as Christians, must learn to follow orders. God wants things in order and beautiful. He was so explicit in His ordering of some things.

Read 1 Corinthians 14:33.

God orders our steps. Whether or not we follow the orders is up to us. Notice His ordering for the Tabernacle, after which His *glory* appeared.

Notice: Have I followed His orders? If so, His *glory* should appear in my life.

PRAYER

> God, I want Your ordering and direction in my life. I do not want to be spiritually deaf to Your order for me. Help me to keep the channel open so I can hear and follow. I desire to experience Your glory personally.

Note: Be cautious to listen closely, because sometimes God does not speak or nudge very strongly. It might be a still, small voice, a slight nudge, or a captive thought. Listen intently.

SPIRITS ON ITEMS

$\mathscr{R}$EAD DEUTERONOMY 7:1–26 (NOTICE VERSES 25 and 26), Deuteronomy 13:15–18, and Proverbs 23:6.

We see so many innocent and pretty looking items sitting around in houses, and in stores for purchasing. I did say innocent looking items. Let us look at it this way. We are taught from the scriptures to anoint people and pray for their healing. Many times, houses are anointed and blessed. All of these are good and right.

Be aware! The devil can enter a house as a curse on items. It is good to anoint and pray over items. Sometimes these spirits manifest through sounds. Do not be afraid. "For God hath not given us the spirit of fear; but of power, and of love, and of a sound mind" (2 Timothy 1:7 KJV).

It was told years ago that the devil was given leeway with heavy metal music. In the world, there are two kinds of spirits: the Holy Spirit and an evil spirit.

Spirits can attach themselves to items. My husband told me once to never borrow things from a particular individual again. The person was so accommodating, gracious, and helpful. Many times, people are not aware of the spirits they have in their houses. Remember, wolves come in sheep's clothing. The devil is sly.

Now, take this time to go through your house and anoint the doorsills and other items, and pray: "God, I pray for the presence of the Holy Spirit to be in my house at all times. I ask You to help me to be very aware of the evil spirit, whether it is on items or in my presence."

UNEQUALLY YOKED

*S*O MANY TIMES, WE HAVE heard messages and conversations that people should not be unequally yoked together. This is particularly applied to marriage. In dating and in marriage, there are times the believer feels he or she can win the person over. This may have happened, but it is a chance to take. Adjustment in marriage alone is enough to deal with. Do not go against the teaching of the scriptures. Two spirits warring against each other is extra conflict.

Read the following: 2 Corinthians 6:14, Ephesians 5:6, 7, and 11, and 1 Timothy 5:22.

Being unequally yoked does not only apply to marriage but in a binding business partnership as well (2 Chronicles 20:35–37) The aim a person has in mind to reach the goal can be entirely different from the other person's view.

The question may be asked, "Should I work for someone who is not a Christian?" How do we always know? If you are working for a boss who wants you to compromise your beliefs, that is a red flag. Stand your ground in a nice way, with respect. If the workplace becomes too intense, it might be a way to move you to another place where you need to be. Also, remember there are seasons in our lives. Once one season has been completed, another one can arise.

Think of Abram. God told him to leave from Ur of the Chaldees and go to the place He would show him. Sometimes it takes being uprooted, and different seasons, to get us to our destinations and release us from situations we should not deal with.

PRAYER

God, I ask for your clear direction in marriage (if single). I want my marriage to be a three-some: God, my spouse, and me. I ask for Your direction in business dealings, with bosses, and in any binding contracts. Help me with decisions I should make.

I AM AN AGENT

*A*N INSURANCE AGENT CAN PERSONALLY put money in the pocket, and give peace in the mind of a buyer.

I am not an insurance agent, but I am an assurance agent. My calling is to speak and promote truth, and help in pointing people to the place where their needs can be met. I am just one of God's agents or representatives, serving as His mouth, hands, and feet.

An assurance agent can receive satisfaction in acting on the responsibility as a Christian, knowing he or she is encouraging peace in the mind of the believer.

In the game tug of war, everyone needs to be strong and give all of his or her energy to pulling on the rope. Think of a chain: every link should be strong, intact, and with no flaws, to prevent breakage.

All Christians are in the army of the Lord and have certain callings and jobs to perform (1 Corinthians 3:6–10 and 2 Corinthians 6:1). Any weakness can affect the performance of another Christian. Ephesians 6:10 tells me what to do. Ephesians 6:11–20 tells me how to do.

An insurance agent would not think of filling that position without being equipped, by studying and gaining knowledge, receiving proper training, and acquiring information to pass on to others. As a Christian, an assurance agent also needs preparation. Experience helps.

In some jobs, bonuses are given as rewards, and can be used as incentives to keep up the good work and improve even more. There are also rewards in doing God's work.

Scriptures to read: Psalm 31:23, Psalm 58:11, Psalm 62:12, Luke 6:35, and 1 Corinthians 15:58.

PRAYER

God, please help me to fill my position well and in a way pleasing to you. I do not want to be a weak link in Your army. I want to pull my load. May I be the agent You can count on.

Geraldine Turner

ANGELS

$\mathcal{M}$UCH HAS BEEN SAID ABOUT angels. An angel is a spiritual being believed to act as an attendant, agent, or messenger of God, represented in human form. Examples of some angels in the scriptures are Michael, Raphael, and Gabriel.

Do you believe that every Christian has a guardian angel?

Read Psalm 34:7, Psalm 91:11–12, Matthew 18:10, and Hebrews 1:13–14.

Some people find comfort in saying that their loved ones who have passed on are angels in Heaven, looking down on them. *Not so!* If this was true, how could they enjoy Heaven if they see the sorrow we are in? In Heaven, all tears are wiped from our eyes.

Human beings have souls that are made for God to inhabit. Angels cannot know about salvation for themselves, but they can minister to us.

I have a friend who said she knows the name of her guardian angel.

Angels appeared to Abraham with a message (Genesis 18:1–15). We may entertain or be in the presence of angels and not realize it (Hebrews 13:2).

Some scriptures about angels include Genesis 32:1–32, Exodus 14:19, Numbers 20:16, Judges 6:11–24, 2 Kings 19:35, and Psalm 148:2.

Not all angels are good; some are evil (Psalm 78:49). Remember, Satan and one third of the angels in Heaven were cast out. Do you know that we will judge angels (1 Corinthians 6:3)?

PRAYER

God, I thank You for my guardian angel and for angels that You send to minister to Your people. Help me to work with them to do my part.

Geraldine Turner

PEER PRESSURE

*T*HE TERM PEER PRESSURE HAS a negative connotation. This can be true, but not always. For example, if your peers (friends) are implementing good habits and choices, they can point you in a positive direction. On the opposite side of that coin, if their ways and habits are not good, their influence is negative. Whichever of these examples, we are affected. It is easy to do good or bad with plenty of support. That is why people are accountable to each other. It can be easy to give in and go along with the crowd rather than to be teased and looked down on. This should be where *the buck stops*.

I have made the statement in the past that I do not have to live with anyone, but I do have to live with myself. At the end of the day, whatever choices I have made can haunt me or make me feel good.

Read 1 Kings 12:1–15 (KJV). Notice verses 8 and 10. Rehoboam's approach was not one of kindness consideration but a flying-off-the-handle kind of reaction, urged by his peers. He refused experience and wisdom from the older ones and went with the hotheaded peers. Read 2 Chronicles 10:1–19.

Be careful in sharing with your peers that they are not directing you for selfish reasons. Remember, at the end of the day it is you and God. Pray and seek God's directions in decisions to be made.

Read Jeremiah 9:23–24, Proverbs 3:5–6, Proverbs 13:10, and Luke 14:31.

PRAYER

God, I so much want to get Your direction in my life, and in decisions I have to make. I thank You for friends who I can use as sounding boards and who can be good influences. May I be so connected with You that I can feel or sense the proper direction to go.

A BEAUTIFUL TEMPLE
(NATURAL, SPIRITUAL)

*R*EAD 1 CHRONICLES 28:9–21.

The scripture tells, in detail, of the temple Solomon was to build. Read 1 Chronicles 29:1–9.

God wanted objects in His temple to be beautiful and eloquent. The temple was by His direction, design, and workmanship. We, as Christians, are His workmanship (Ephesians 2:10). God wants things done decently and in order. Take note of these scriptures: Deuteronomy 22:11, 2 Chronicles 3:6, Ezekiel 44:17–18, 1 Corinthians 3:16–17, 1 Corinthians 6:19–20, and 2 Corinthians 6:16.

We are given direction in Romans 12:1. The scriptures speak of different parts of the body. For example, "The light of the body is the eye" (Luke 11:34 KJV). The scriptures also speak of having a pure, clean, and new *heart*, and new spirit. They tell us not to have a heart that is fearful, hardened, or stony. Another part of our temple is our *hands*, which we are told to keep *clean*. *Feet* are also mentioned (Romans 10:15).

Every part of my body/temple should be clean, in order, and pleasing to God. I must hide God's Word in my heart so I can keep my temple clean. The Word says that whatever comes out of a heart defiles the person, so I must feed it good data.

Other scriptures on the subject of the heart are these: 1 Samuel 16:7, Proverbs 4:23, Matthew 5:8, Ephesians 1:18, Philippians 4:7, and James 4:8.

This devotion refers to the natural temple that Solomon built and the spiritual temples, our bodies, that we are responsible for.

PRAYER

God, I ask You to help me to keep my temple clean
for You to inhabit, with workmanship that will please
You, and as a living sacrifice, holy and acceptable.

Geraldine Turner

MUSIC, SINGING, PRAISING WON THE BATTLE

*R*EAD 2 CHRONICLES 20:1–30. NOTICE verse 21. Jehoshaphat appointed singers, but not just to sing. The scripture says he appointed singers unto the Lord to praise the beauty of holiness and to say, "Praise the Lord; for His mercy endureth forever" (Psalm 136:1–26 KJV). When they began to sing and praise, the Lord set ambushments against their enemies and they were winners.

Singing and praising the Lord in worship is so important that some were appointed for this task day and night (1Chronicles 9:33). Anointed music is powerful!

Read 1 Samuel 16:14–23, 2 Samuel 22:1–51 (note verse 50), and Joshua 6:20.

It is noted in the scriptures of ways God worked through singing and praising. It worked for them and should work for us. Sometimes personal battles are so hard. Be careful not to give the battle more attention than the one who fights the battle for us. Wear the *garment of praise* for the spirit of heaviness (Isaiah 61:1–3).

Suggestion: Just before praying and worshipping, put on praise and worship music.

Read Acts 16:25–26, Psalm 103:1–5, and Psalm 150:1–6.

PRAYER

> God, I praise You for Who You are; for showing up in my battles, I give You thanks. You are worthy to be praised and honored. I do not want to withhold the praise that You deserve. I love You, I worship You, I bless You.

Take this time to worship and love God in your own way.

LET THE WORD OF CHRIST DWELL IN YOU RICHLY

*T*HE INTENTION OF EVERY DEVOTION in this book has been to get an individual in the Word and the Word in the individual. For what purpose?

> "Thy Word have I hid in mine heart, that I might not sin against thee" (Psalm 119:11 KJV).

> "Let the Word of Christ Dwell In You Richly" (Colossians 3:16–17 KJV).

In the natural, we need lights to guide us. There is no reason to live life in a spiritually blind condition, therefore, we have the Word (Psalm 119:105 KJV). "Thy Word is a lamp unto my feet, and a light unto my path." The lamp is closer to the subject, the feet. The light is an overall view of the path. We need both.

Proverbs 6:23 (KJV) says, "For the commandment is a lamp; and the law is light; and reproofs of instruction are the way of life." Once again, the commandment is a lamp which shows the subject, and the law is the overall light.

Romans 10:17 (KJV) says that faith comes by hearing the Word. We cannot please God without faith, and we cannot have faith without the Word.

James 1:23–25 (KJV) says to be a hearer and a doer.

First John 2:5 (KJV) says to be a keeper of the Word.

Psalm 19:8 (KJV) says that the statutes and commandments of the Lord are right.

Second Timothy 2:15 (KJV) says, "Study to show thyself approved unto God, a workman that needeth not to be ashamed, rightly dividing the word of truth."

Reading/hearing God's Word and placing it in our minds and hearts gives us authority to speak His Word, and thereby gain miracles.

Worship brings God's presence to us.

PRAYER

God, I thank You for giving us the living Word, Jesus, and the written Word. I ask You to help me to store the Word in me and uphold it, because it is my roadmap to Heaven. I love You and thank You for being God Almighty.

Geraldine Turner

Printed in the United States
by Baker & Taylor Publisher Services